Includes a Have a Bully-Free Day! skit!

Ha, ha, Teddy!

By Jeannette Sabatini

ISBN-10: 0692571558
ISBN-13: 978-0692571552

Dedication

This book is dedicated to children everywhere and to my family, particularly my husband and sons, who are inspirational and supportive.

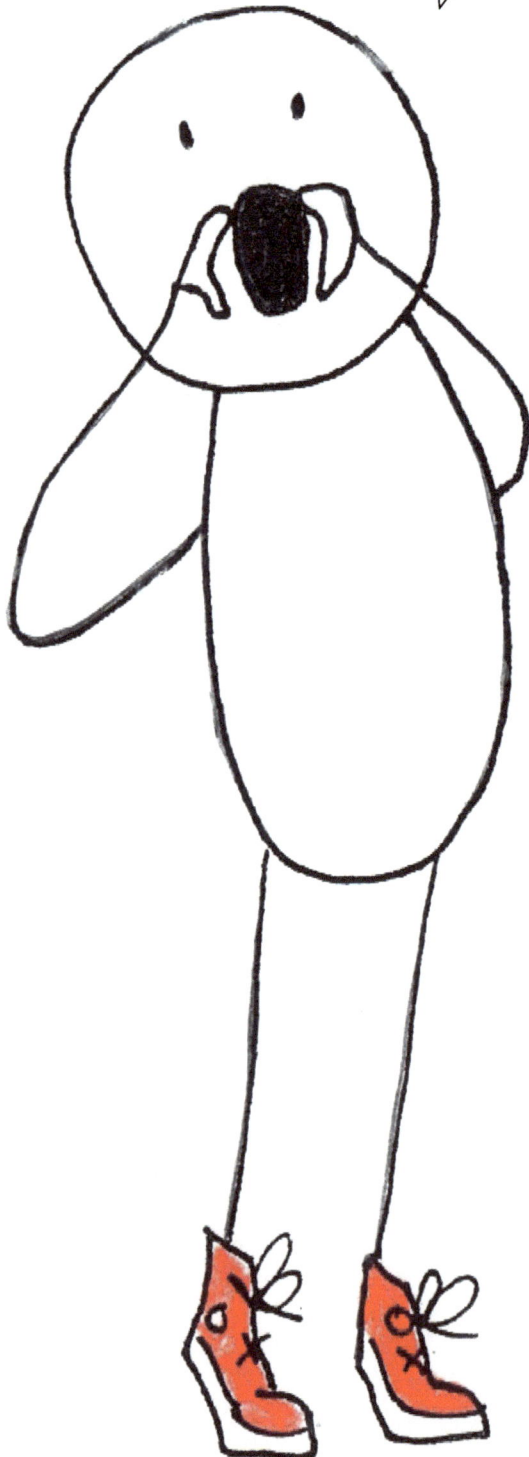

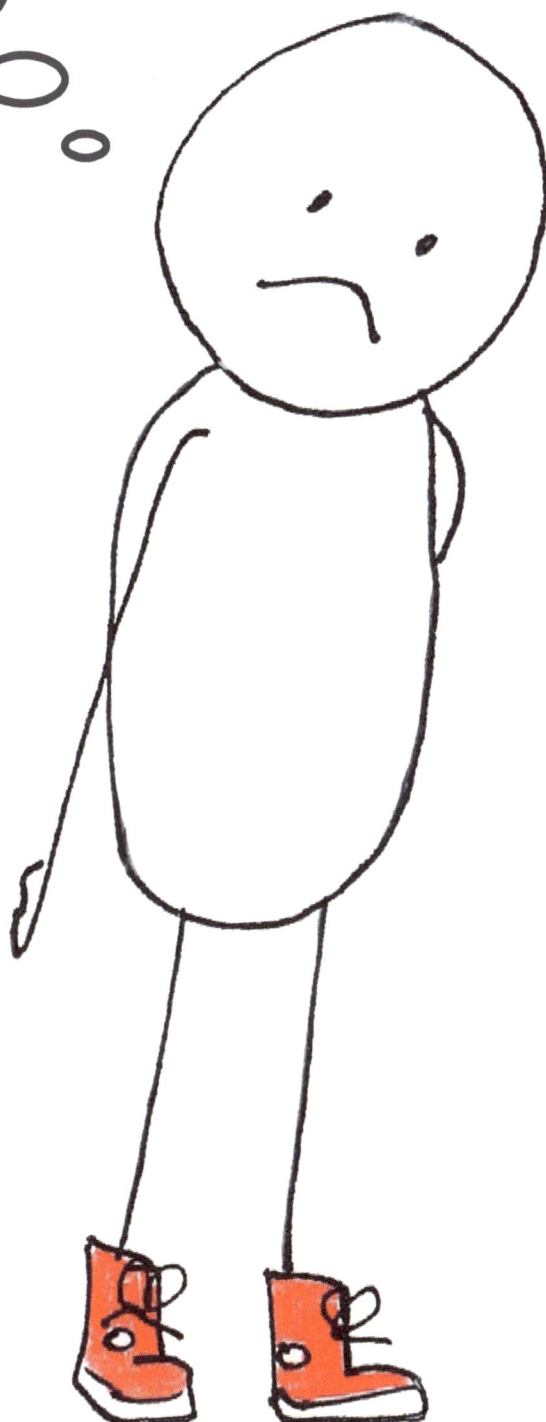

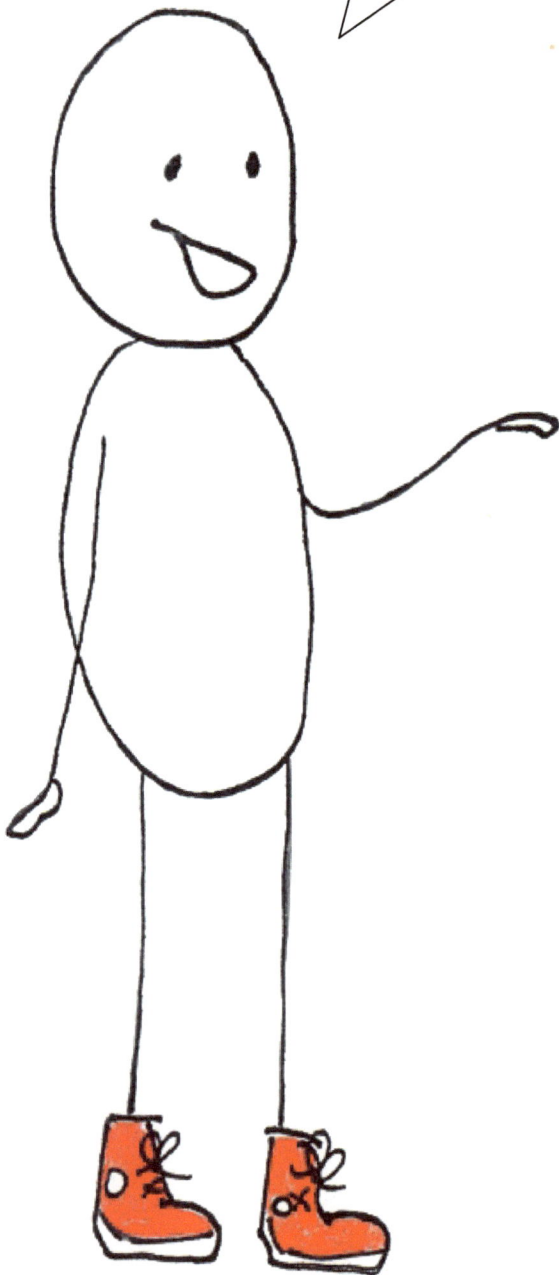

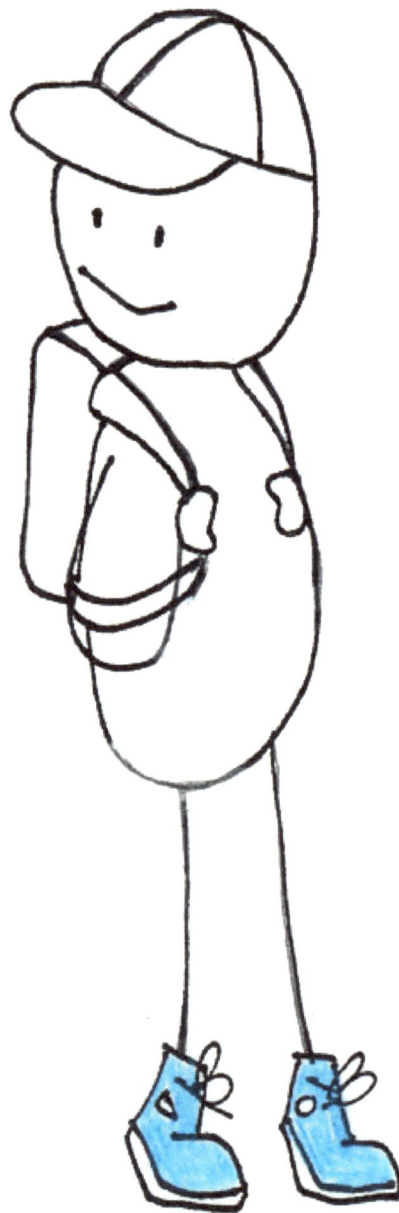

Teddy, listen...I'm coming clean!
I said things that were mean.
Teddy, may I be your friend?
As far as bullying...I'm done, the end!

Try This "Have a Bully-Free Day!" Skit!!

Kids will love acting out this skit, "Three's Not a Crowd," from "Have a Bully-Free Day! Short Skits for Children," to be available soon. The situation presented is a common one: A child makes a friend but then tightens that bond to the point that he or she is threatened by any other child who wants to join in. Close friendships are great, but kids can miss out on other meaningful relationships if they keep others out.

Some Helpful Tips To Use Prior to Your Performance

- This skit is based on a poem that is printed on the opposite page. The skit reads somewhat differently than the poem because it was tweaked to benefit the performance.
- Make copies of the skit for each actor and have them highlight their lines using individual colors.
- Prior to the show, introduce the actors and the character each will play. Consider having each actor wear a nametag showing his or her character's name.
- Don't rush the performance! The skit will take about as long as a commercial to perform.
- Get the audience involved! Ask them if they have a personal connection with the message (remind kids to leave names out of stories they share). Actors can share personal experiences, as well!

THREE'S NOT A CROWD
By Jeannette Sabatini

My one friend at school used to be Jim.
I liked it when it was just me and him.
Out on the blacktop we liked to play ball.
We had no need for the others at all.
At lunch every day, I'd save Jim a seat.
Then came along this new kid named Pete.
He sat down beside me. I gave him a look.
"Hey, kid!" I said, "That's Jim's seat you took!"
"There're plenty of spots," Pete said with a grin.
I didn't like this. Pete was under my skin.
When Jim showed up, I didn't know what to say.
He parked next to Pete, who was ruining my day.
To my surprise, Jim greeted Pete with a "Yo!"
If I had the nerve, I'd tell Pete to just go!
We ate in silence; a bite, then a slurp.
Then without warning, Pete let out a burp!
I couldn't help laughing! Milk came out my nose!
The lunch lady barked: "Now look at your clothes!"
Pete was laughing so hard he let out a toot.
I couldn't resist saying, "That was a beaut!"
Jim sounded off farts into the palm of his hand.
These things are outlawed...in school they are banned!
Yes, we were rowdy. You bet we were loud.
Yet I learned that day that three's not a crowd.
Pete's pretty cool. He sure makes us laugh.
If he has a cookie, he'll give anyone half.
Now out at recess, Pete joins in our game.
Things are more fun when they're not always the same.

SKIT: THREE'S NOT A CROWD

ABOUT THE PARTS:

- **INTRO PERSON (speaking part):** This person reads the intro and closing comments. He/she also introduces each actor and their roles.

- **NARRATOR (speaking part):** This person provides some extra details throughout the skit.

- **RAJ (speaking & acting):** This person is the main character who does most of the talking and acting throughout the play.

- **JIM (speaking & acting):** Raj's original buddy.

- **PETE (speaking & acting):** The person who is viewed as a threat.

- **LUNCH LADY:** This person has one line to be said loudly and clearly.

- **EXTRAS:** These actors are used to give character to the scene.

PROPS NEEDED:

- _Chairs_
- _Ball_
- _Whoopee cushion (inflated, ready to use)_
- _Lunch Lady costume (wig, hairnet, apron, spoon)_
- _Lunchboxes (2)_
- _Lunch tray with fake lunch food_
- _Apple_

SETTING THE FIRST SCENE: IN THE PLAYGROUND

➢ _Group of Actors: Each is involved in a playground activity: jump rope, four-square, tag, etc._

➢ _Raj and Jim: They are center stage having a catch with a ball._

➢ _Intro Person: Comes on stage and introduces each actor and the role each will play. Exits the stage after saying the following line:_

Intro Person (exits after saying the following):
Do you have a special friend? Do you only do things with that friend? Maybe you swing on the swings together every day or toss a ball at lunch on the playground. How would you feel if someone else came along and asked to play? Would you say "No!" or "Sure!"?

PERFORMANCE BEGINS
SCENE 1: THE PLAYGROUND

Raj:
My one friend at school used to be Jim.

➤ *Jim comes out with a ball and stands next to Raj.*

Raj:
 I liked it when it was just me and him.
 Out on the blacktop we liked to play ball.

➤ *Raj and Jim have a catch. Soon, Raj holds the ball, faces the audience and says:*

Raj:
 We had no need for the others at all.

➤ *Raj and Jim throw the ball a few more times and then Jim exits with the ball.*

SCENE 2: THE LUNCHROOM

➤ *SET UP: Three chairs are placed in row, facing the audience. A ball has been placed behind one of the chairs. The lunchbox to be used by Raj contains the apple while the one Pete will use contains the inflated whoopee cushion.*

Narrator:
 At lunch every day, Raj would save Jim a seat.

➤ *Raj comes in holding his lunchbox. He sits in the chair on far left. He takes the apple out of his lunchbox and puts it on the middle seat, like he is saving the seat.*

Narrator:
Then came along this new kid named Pete.

➢ *Pete (with lunchbox) enters, hands apple to Raj and takes the middle seat.*

Narrator:
He sat down beside Raj, who gave him a look.

Raj (looking annoyed at Pete):
Hey!...

Narrator (looking at audience:
...Raj continued...

Raj (to Pete, still annoyed):
That's Jim's seat you took!

Pete (smiling):
There're plenty of spots!...

Narrator (to the audience):
...Pete said with a grin. Raj didn't like this. Pete was under his skin.

➢ *Pete is smiling; Raj is not. Jim enters (with lunch tray) amd stands in front of empty seat.*

Narrator:
When Jim showed up, Raj didn't know what to say.
He parked next to Pete, who was ruining Raj's day.
To Raj's surprise, Jim greeted Pete with a: "Yo!"

Jim (to Pete):
Yo!

Raj (annoyed, to the audience):
If I had the nerve I'd tell Pete to just go!

Narrator:
They ate in silence; a bite, then a slurp.
Then without warning, Pete let out a burp!

➢ *Pete fakes a loud burp. Raj responds with laughter.*

Narrator:
Raj couldn't help laughing! Milk came out his nose!
The lunch lady barked...

➢ *Lunch Lady stomps over to them and points at each one of them with a spoon.*

Lunch Lady:
Now look at your clothes!

Narrator:
Pete was laughing so hard he let out a toot!

➢ *Pete takes the whoopee cushion out of his lunchbox and sits on it. They all laugh.*

Narrator:
Raj couldn't resist saying…

Raj:
That was a beaut!

Narrator:
Jim sounded off farts into the palm of his hand.
These things are outlawed…in school they are banned!

➢ *Jim sounds off a few fart noises into the palm of his hand. After that, Raj stands up and talks to the audience.*

Raj:
Yes, we were rowdy! You bet we were loud!
Yet that day I learned that three's not a crowd.

➢ *Jim stands up and talks to the audience. Raj is still standing.*

<u>Jim:</u>
Pete's pretty cool. He sure makes us laugh.
If he has a cookie, he'll give anyone half.

➢ *Pete now stands up and the three boys put their arms around each others '
shoulders. While in this position, Raj speaks:*

<u>Raj:</u>
Now out at recess, Pete joins in our game.
Things are more fun when they're not always the same!

➢ *The three boys drop their arms so Raj can go behind the chair to grab the ball.
The three boys have a catch with it . Intro Person enters the scene and talks to
the audience.*

<u>Intro Person:</u>
We may be tempted to keep others out of our group of friends. This skit shows
us what can happen when we are not afraid to welcome others to play: we can
make a new, awesome friend!

About "Have a Bully-Free Day!" Books

Have a Bully-Free Day! books are written to help children have a bully-free day every day at school or in the neighborhood. They build empathy and compassion and explain the rewards of being nice and the consequences of being mean. *Have a Bully-Free Day!* books help children:

- realize how negative behavior can impact friendships
- see the benefits of being friendly and positive
- welcome others into friendships
- stop seeing other kids as a threat
- deal with a person who is bullying
- be sensitive to the circumstances of others
- notice the physical signs that they have hurt another's feelings.

Kids enjoy these books because they relate to the situations presented and they enjoy the fun rhyming pattern in each. They are great for sharing: teachers can share them with a class, a counselor with a group or individual, and students with other students. Older children will enjoy acting out the skit for younger children.

The author, Jeannette Sabatini, is a writer and illustrator with a degree in English/Journalism. She has been an editor and writer in the medical field, but her experience as a mom and an elementary school aide inspired her to start writing and illustrating stories for children. She expresses her motherly advice through poetry.

This and other *Have a Bully-Free Day!* books are available on Amazon Books.